AI Side Income Mastery :

Your Guide to Earning Extra Income In the Age of Artificial Intelligence

-Amit Gupta

Disclaimer

This book is for educational and informational purposes only. The strategies, prompts, and examples provided are intended to help readers explore side income opportunities using AI tools.

- ❖ No Financial Guarantee: Results may vary depending on effort, skills, and market conditions. This is not a "get-rich-quick" guide.
- ❖ AI Trading: Any mention of trading with AI is strictly educational. Trading involves risk, and you should consult a licensed financial advisor before investing real money.Never invest money you cannot afford to lose.
- ❖ Ethical Use: Please use AI responsibly. Do not use it for plagiarism, spreading misinformation, or any harmful activity.

Always do your own due diligence and consult professionals when necessary.

By reading further, you accept full responsibility for your choices, actions, and outcomes.

Copyright

➢ Published by Amit Kumar Gupta

Table of Content

Introduction – Why AI is the Biggest Wealth Shift of Our Time

Imagine waking up in the morning, grabbing your coffee, and instead of rushing to a job you dislike, you spend 1–2 hours creating something valuable with the help of AI—maybe a blog post, a design for a T-shirt, or even a short script for YouTube. Later that day, while you're at work, spending time with family, or even sleeping, that creation is out there in the world earning you money.

This isn't a fantasy anymore. It's happening right now.

A Personal Touch

I still remember the first time I used AI to create content. I typed a simple prompt into a chatbot and within seconds it gave me a polished article draft. I wasn't a professional writer, yet I felt like one. That moment changed how I saw technology—not as something complicated and reserved for experts, but as a *partner* that could help me earn, create, and grow.

AI is not just for Silicon Valley or tech geniuses. It's for you. For the single mom who wants to earn extra income from home. For the student looking to build a portfolio. For the retiree who wants to turn hobbies into earnings. For the busy employee who dreams of having financial freedom.

We are living through the **biggest wealth shift in history**, where ordinary people can leverage extraordinary tools.

Why You Should Read This Book

This book is not about theories. It's about **practical, actionable steps** to generate side income with AI—even if you have no tech skills.

Here's what you'll discover inside:

- How to use AI to create content, designs, books, and products
- How to freelance smarter (not harder) with AI as your silent teammate
- How to explore digital products, consulting, and even trading (responsibly)
- Real stories of people like you who've done it
- A **60-Day Action Plan** to kickstart your AI-powered income journey

Setting Expectations

Let's be honest: AI is powerful, but it's not magic. You won't get rich overnight. This book is about building **realistic, reliable streams of income** that can grow over time. Think of it as planting seeds today that can grow into a forest of opportunities tomorrow.

If you're ready to learn, experiment, and take action, AI can truly transform your financial life.

Chapter 1: Understanding AI in Simple Words

The Fear and the Mystery Around AI

If you've ever heard words like **Artificial Intelligence, machine learning, or neural networks** and felt your head spin — you're not alone.

AI often sounds complicated, and many people assume it's only for scientists, engineers, or big tech companies. The truth? AI has already slipped into your daily life quietly:

- When Netflix suggests a movie you might like → That's AI.
- When Google Maps reroutes you because of traffic → That's AI.
- When your phone autocorrects a misspelled word → That's AI.

Now, with tools like **ChatGPT, MidJourney, Canva AI, and others**, you can directly use AI to create, write, design, and even brainstorm ideas — without needing to code a single line.

What Exactly is AI? (In Plain English)

Artificial Intelligence (AI) simply means:

👉 A computer program that can "think" or "decide" like a human for specific tasks.

It doesn't have emotions or consciousness, but it can **analyze patterns, learn from data, and generate results faster than humans.**

Think of AI as:

★ A super-fast assistant who never sleeps.

★ A brainstorming partner who always has ideas.

★ A productivity booster who reduces your work from hours to minutes.

Why AI is Perfect for Side Hustles

In the past, starting a side hustle required:

➢ Specialized skills (graphic design, coding, writing expertise).
➢ Significant time investment.

➢ Sometimes, upfront money.

But now AI can:

➢ **Write:** Draft blog posts, social media captions, YouTube scripts.

➢ **Design:**Create logos, posters, T-shirt designs, book covers.

➢ **Research:** Find trending topics, keywords, and market opportunities.

➢ **Automate:** Handle repetitive tasks like customer replies, email sorting, or summarizing reports.

This means anyone — even with little experience — can use AI as a lever to **skip the hard, boring parts** and focus on creativity and execution.

The Tools You Should Know

Let's keep it simple. Here are some beginner-friendly AI tools you'll meet often in this book:

1. ChatGPT (or any AI chatbot)

- Your writing, brainstorming, and problem-solving assistant.

2. MidJourney / DALL·E / Stable Diffusion

- AI tools that generate art and images.

3. Canva AI

- An easy design platform with AI-powered suggestions.

4. Notion AI

- Organizes your work, generates summaries, helps in productivity.

5. AI Voice & Video Tools (like Descript, ElevenLabs, Pictory)

- Convert text into videos or voiceovers.

💡 AI Prompt Box – Discover the Right Tools

Try asking ChatGPT:

"List 5 beginner-friendly AI tools for side hustles, explain in one line what each does, and give me free alternatives if possible."

This way you'll instantly discover tools (and their free versions) that fit your budget and goals.

Example: From Zero to Blog Post in 10 Minutes

Let's say you want to start a blog about **healthy recipes for busy people**. In the past, you'd need to spend hours researching, drafting, and editing.

Now, watch how AI can help:

Prompt Example for ChatGPT:

"Write a 700-word blog post on *5 Quick and Healthy Breakfast Ideas for Busy Mornings*. Keep the tone friendly, practical, and easy for beginners. Suggest simple ingredients and add a short motivational intro."

Within seconds, AI will generate a draft. You can then polish it, add your personal touch (like your favorite oatmeal recipe), and hit publish.

💡 **AI Prompt Box – Blog Starter Pack**

- "Suggest 10 blog post titles for \[your niche]. Make them catchy and beginner-friendly."
- "Write a blog outline on \[topic]. Include introduction, main points, and conclusion."
- "Rewrite this paragraph to make it more engaging and conversational: \[paste text]."

Common Myths About AI

1. "AI will replace me."

- Reality: AI won't replace you. But people who use AI *will* replace those who don't.

2. "I need to learn coding to use AI."

- Reality: You don't. Most AI tools today are as simple as chatting with a friend or clicking a few buttons.

3. "AI is cheating or inauthentic."

- Reality: AI is a tool. Just like a calculator helps you do math faster, AI helps you create faster. The value still comes from **your ideas, creativity, and how you use it.**

Practical Exercise

💡 AI Prompt Box – Idea Generator

"Give me 5 creative side hustle ideas that someone with no special skills but 2 hours a day could start using AI."

👉 Action Step: Write down the 1–2 ideas that excite you the most. This will be your first spark for building an AI side hustle.

Chapter Summary

- AI is not some scary robot—it's simply smart software that helps you work faster.
- It's already around you, and now it's in your hands.
- You don't need to be technical to use AI. You just need curiosity and the right prompts.
- Think of AI as your **sidekick** in the journey of creating side income.

Chapter 2: Mindset for AI Side Hustles

Why Mindset Matters More Than Tools

When people first discover AI tools, they often get excited for a few days, play around, and then... stop. Why?

It's not because the tools don't work. It's because of **mindset**.

The truth is:

- **AI can give you ideas, but you must take action.**
- **AI can save you time, but you must stay consistent.**
- **AI can open doors, but you must walk through them.**

Your mindset is the fuel that turns AI from "**just a tool**" into a **life-changing income partner**.

The Employee Mindset vs. The Side Hustler Mindset

Most of us are raised with the idea: Study hard, get a job, and earn a salary. That's the **employee mindset**.

But side hustles — especially AI-powered ones — need a different way of thinking:

- **Employee Mindset:** Wait for instructions.
- **Side Hustler Mindset:** Create opportunities.

- **Employee Mindset:** Earn from one source (salary).
- **Side Hustler Mindset:** Build multiple income streams.
- **Employee Mindset:** Fear of mistakes.
- **Side Hustler Mindset:** Learn from experiments.

With AI, you don't need to be an expert. You just need curiosity and the courage to try.

Overcoming Self-Doubt

It's normal to think:

- "I'm not creative enough."
- "I don't know how to use AI properly."
- "What if I fail?"

Here's the truth: **Everyone feels this way at the beginning**.

The difference is: successful people **start small, experiment, and grow.**

💡 AI Prompt Box – Confidence Boost

Try this with ChatGPT:

"Act as my motivational coach. Remind me why it's never too late to start something new, and give me 5 reasons I'm capable of building an AI side hustle."

Reading encouraging words tailored to you can silence self-doubt and keep you moving.

Curiosity is the Secret Ingredient

AI is like a magic box. The more curious you are, the more treasures you'll find.

Here's a simple formula:

👉 **Curiosity + AI Prompts = Endless Opportunities**

For example:

- ❖ Curious about fitness? → Use AI to create a workout guide.
- ❖ Curious about travel? → Use AI to build a blog about hidden gems.
- ❖ Curious about business? → Use AI to research profitable niches.

💡 **AI Prompt Box – Curiosity Explorer**
Ask ChatGPT:

"Give me 10 creative side hustle ideas combining AI with my interest in \[insert your hobby/interest]. Rank them from easiest to hardest to start."

Action Step: Pick one idea that excites you. Don't worry about it being perfect — just start.

Building the Experiment Habit

One powerful mindset shift:

👉 **Don't think of AI side hustles as pass/fail. Think of them as experiments.**

Instead of saying, "What if I fail?" say, "What will I learn?"

Example:

- You try making an AI-designed T-shirt → Nobody buys it → You learn what designs don't work.
- You publish an AI blog post → Only 10 readers → You learn which topics don't attract people.

Every "failure" is actually **data for your next attempt**.

💡 AI Prompt Box – Small Wins Planner

Ask ChatGPT:

"I want to build an AI-powered side hustle, but I have only 2 hours per day. Suggest a 7-day plan with small, doable steps that will give me tiny wins and keep me motivated."

This way, you'll always focus on progress, not perfection.

Chapter Summary

- AI is powerful, but mindset is the key that unlocks it.
- Shift from the **employee mindset** (waiting, fearing mistakes) to the **side hustler mindset** (creating, experimenting).
- Overcome self-doubt with small wins and motivation.
- Curiosity will fuel your ideas, and experiments will teach you what works.

Chapter 3: Freelancing with AI Support

Why Freelancing is the Fastest Path to Side Income

Freelancing is one of the quickest ways to start earning with AI because:

- You don't need to build a website or brand from scratch.
- Clients are already searching for services on platforms like **Fiverr, Upwork, and Freelancer.**
- With AI, you can deliver professional-quality work in a fraction of the time.

All you need is:

1. A profile that looks trustworthy.
2. A clear description of what you offer.
3. The ability to use AI to complete tasks quickly.

What Services Can You Offer Using AI?

Here are beginner-friendly freelancing services powered by AI:

1. Content Writing

- Blog posts, website copy, product descriptions, email newsletters.
- AI helps with brainstorming, drafting, and editing.

2. Graphic Design

- Social media posts, T-shirt designs, logos, presentations.
- Use Canva AI or MidJourney to create professional visuals.

3. Video & Audio Services

- Voiceovers (using ElevenLabs).
- Subtitles, podcast editing (using Descript or AI captioning).

4. Virtual Assistance

- Customer email replies, research, scheduling.
- AI tools like ChatGPT and Notion make tasks faster.

5. SEO & Research

- Keyword research, competitor analysis, blog outlines.
- AI tools generate reports in minutes.

💡 AI Prompt Box – Freelance Service Finder

Ask ChatGPT:

"Based on the skills of a beginner who has no coding knowledge but wants to use AI, suggest 10 freelance services they can offer on Fiverr or Upwork. Rank them by how easy they are to start."

👉 Action Step: Pick one service that feels easiest and most fun to you.

Sample Gig Descriptions (Copy-Paste Friendly)

Here are **ready-to-use gig templates** you can adapt for Fiverr or Upwork:

1. Blog Writing with AI Assistance

Title:
"I will write high-quality blog posts and articles using AI-powered research"

Description:
Looking for engaging, SEO-friendly blog posts? I use advanced AI tools combined with human creativity to deliver well-structured, polished articles tailored to your audience. You'll get:

- ■ 100% original content (AI-assisted, human-edited)
- SEO optimization with keywords
- A professional tone (casual, formal, or friendly)
- Fast delivery

Prompt to use in ChatGPT:

"Write a 1000-word SEO-friendly blog post on *\[topic]*. Include an engaging introduction, 5 main points with subheadings, and a conclusion. Suggest meta description and 5 keyword-rich titles."

2. Social Media Content Creation

Title:
"I will create eye-catching social media posts and captions using AI design tools"

Description:

Need daily content for Instagram, Facebook, or LinkedIn? I combine AI design platforms like Canva AI with creative strategy to deliver posts that stand out. What you'll get:

- ■ 5–10 ready-to-post designs
- Catchy captions and hashtags
- Consistent brand style
- Quick turnaround

Prompt to use in ChatGPT:

"Generate 10 creative Instagram captions for a \[business type, e.g., fitness coach]. Each caption should be short, engaging, and include a call-to-action and 3 relevant hashtags."

Prompt for Canva AI:

"Create a clean, modern Instagram post about \[topic]. Use minimal design and bold text for attention."

3. T-Shirt or Print-on-Demand Design

Title:
"I will design custom AI-generated T-shirt graphics for your brand"

Description:
Want unique T-shirt designs that pop? I use advanced AI art tools (like MidJourney) to create high-quality, print-ready designs. Perfect for personal use or print-on-demand stores. You'll get:

- AI-generated, original designs
- High-resolution files (PNG, 300dpi)
- Unlimited creativity in style & theme

Prompt for MidJourney:

"Minimalist T-shirt design featuring a retro sunset and silhouette of a surfer, vector style, bold lines, simple color palette."

4. SEO Research & Optimization

Title:
"I will do AI-powered keyword research and SEO blog outlines"

Description:
Struggling to find the right keywords? I use AI-driven research to generate a list of profitable keywords, blog post ideas, and SEO-friendly outlines. Perfect for bloggers and businesses who want traffic fast.

Prompt to use in ChatGPT:

"Generate 20 blog post ideas around \[niche]. Suggest 5 keywords for each, and create a blog outline for the top 3 with SEO optimization."

How Much Can You Charge?

- Blog posts (500–1000 words): **$15– $50** depending on quality and niche.
- Social media post bundles (10 designs + captions): **$20–$100.**
- T-shirt designs: **$5–$20 per design.**
- SEO keyword research report: **$25–$100.**

Tip: Start with lower prices to build reviews, then increase as you gain credibility.

Real Example:

Meet Sarah, a college student who loved social media. She created a **Fiverr gig** offering "10 Instagram posts with captions." Using **Canva AI + ChatGPT**, she delivered polished content in 2–3 hours. Within her first month, she earned $250 — money that paid for her groceries and phone bills.

She didn't need to be a designer or a writer. She just needed **AI + consistency.**

💡 AI Prompt Box – Freelance Pitch Creator

Ask ChatGPT:

"Write a Fiverr gig description for someone offering \[service]. Make it sound professional, friendly, and unique. Include 3 package options (basic, standard, premium) with suggested pricing."

Chapter Summary

- Freelancing is the fastest way to start earning with AI.
- You can offer services like content writing, design, SEO, and social media.
- AI reduces workload, speeds up delivery, and improves quality.
- Start small, build reviews, then scale up your pricing.
- Every gig description should be clear, friendly, and benefit-driven.

Chapter 4: AI + Content Creation for Social Media

Why Social Media is a Goldmine for Side Income

Social media isn't just for scrolling and memes anymore — it's a global stage. Millions of people are earning by creating **Instagram posts, YouTube Shorts, TikToks, or motivational reels**.

The best part?

- You don't need expensive cameras or a big team.
- AI tools can help you **write, design, edit, and even generate videos** in minutes.
- You can start for **free** with just your phone + AI.

Different Ways to Earn with Social Media

1. YouTube & YouTube Shorts

- Monetize with ads once you reach **1,000 subscribers + 4,000 watch hours** (or 10 million Shorts views in 90 days).
- Use AI to script videos, create voiceovers, and even edit visuals.

2. TikTok / Instagram Reels

- Monetize through brand deals, sponsored posts, or affiliate marketing.

- AI makes short, catchy content much easier to produce.

3. Instagram / Pinterest Posts

- Build an audience around a niche → sell digital products, offer coaching, or promote affiliate products.

How AI Helps Content Creators

AI can handle the "**hard**" parts of content creation:

- ❖ **Ideas:** Generate video topics, captions, and hashtags.
- ❖ **Scripts:**Write YouTube or TikTok scripts in minutes.
- ❖ **Editing:**AI tools can cut videos, add captions, and polish them.
- ❖ **Voiceovers:**Convert text to natural human-like voice.
- ❖ **Thumbnails & Graphics:**Canva AI or MidJourney create eye-catching visuals.

💡 AI Prompt Box – Content Idea Generator

Ask ChatGPT:

"Suggest 20 viral YouTube Shorts ideas for \[your niche]. Make them beginner-friendly and easy to shoot with a phone. Include catchy titles and hooks."

👉 Action Step: Pick 3 ideas and note them down.

Workflow Example: Creating a Motivational YouTube Short

Let's walk through a **real example** step by step.

1. Generate the Script (ChatGPT)
Prompt:

- "Write a 30-second motivational script about never giving up, in an energetic and uplifting tone. Add a catchy opening line."

2. Create Voiceover (ElevenLabs or Speechify)

- Copy the script and generate a professional-sounding voiceover.

3. Add Video Clips (Pexels, Pixabay, or Pictory AI)

- Use free stock footage (e.g., sunrise, people working out).
- Or use AI tools like Pictory to auto-generate video from text.

4. Add Captions (CapCut or Descript)

- Upload the video → auto captions → style them.

5. **Create Thumbnail (Canva AI or MidJourney)**
Prompt:

"Minimal YouTube thumbnail design: bold motivational quote, dark background, glowing text effect."

👉 Within 1 hour, you have a professional Short ready to upload!

💡 AI Prompt Box – Script Writer
Ask ChatGPT:

"Write a 45-second YouTube Short script for \[niche]. Make it engaging, conversational, and end with a call-to-action like 'Follow for more.'"

Example: Instagram Post Workflow

Let's say you run a fitness Instagram account.

1. **Ask AI for Post Ideas**
   Prompt:

"Generate 10 Instagram post ideas about home workouts for busy professionals. Suggest caption ideas and hashtags."

2. **Design with Canva AI**
   Prompt in Canva AI:

"Create a bold Instagram carousel about '5 Quick Home Exercises.' Use modern fonts and high-contrast colors."

3. **Write Captions with ChatGPT**
   Prompt:

"Write 5 catchy Instagram captions about staying fit at home. Keep them under 100 words and add hashtags."

4. **Post Consistently**
   Schedule with tools like Buffer or Later.

💡 AI Prompt Box – Hashtag Helper
Ask ChatGPT:

“Suggest 20 trending Instagram hashtags for \[niche]. Mix high-traffic and medium-traffic hashtags for best reach.”

Monetization Strategies

Once you start posting consistently and gain followers, here’s how you can earn:

- **Ad Revenue (YouTube Shorts/long videos).**
- **Affiliate Marketing (Amazon Associates, ClickBank, Impact).**
- **Digital Products (guides, templates, courses).**
- **Brand Deals (sponsorships once you have audience trust).**

Real Example

David, a 19-year-old student, started a **motivational YouTube Shorts channel**. Using **ChatGPT for scripts + Pexels stock videos + CapCut captions**, he posted 3 videos per week. In 3 months, he hit **10,000 subscribers**. He hasn’t quit college, but now makes **$300–500/month** in ad revenue + affiliate links.

His secret? **Consistency + AI shortcuts.**

💡 AI Prompt Box – 30-Day Social Media Plan

Ask ChatGPT:

“Create a 30-day content calendar for my \[niche] Instagram account. Include daily post ideas, captions, and hashtags. Make it easy to execute with free tools.”

Chapter Summary

- ❖ Social media is one of the fastest-growing ways to earn side income.
- ❖ AI makes it easy to generate **ideas, scripts, designs, captions, and hashtags**
- ❖ Workflows: YouTube Shorts, Instagram posts, TikTok reels can all be done with AI support.
- ❖ Monetization comes from ads, affiliates, products, and brand deals.
- ❖ The real key = **Consistency.** AI saves time, but posting regularly builds trust.

Chapter 5: Blogging & SEO with AI

Why Blogging Still Works in 2025

Some people think blogging is "**dead**" because of YouTube, TikTok, and Instagram. But here's the truth:

- **Millions of people still search Google daily** for answers.
- Blogs can **earn money passively** through ads and affiliate links.
- With AI, writing blog posts is faster and easier than ever.

Blogging is like planting seeds: it may take 3–6 months to grow, but once your posts start ranking, they bring traffic (and income) 24/7.

Different Ways Blogs Make Money

1. Display Ads (Google AdSense, Mediavine)

- Example: You get 10,000 visitors → \$100– \$200 per month.

2. Affiliate Marketing

- Example: Write a blog post about "Best Laptops for Students." Add Amazon affiliate links → earn commission for every sale.

3. Digital Products

- Example: Sell your own eBook, templates, or courses via your blog.

4. Email List Building

- Collect readers' emails → promote products or services directly.

Choosing a Profitable Niche with AI

Picking the right niche is 50% of blogging success. It must be something people search for + can be monetized.

💡 AI Prompt Box – Niche Research
Ask ChatGPT:

"List 10 profitable blog niches with low competition and high affiliate potential. For each, suggest 3 example blog post titles."

👉 Action Step: Pick a niche you're genuinely curious about (fitness, travel, parenting, tech, etc.).

How AI Can Write Blog Posts

Instead of spending hours writing, AI can generate:

Outlines

Blog drafts

SEO titles & meta descriptions

Engaging introductions

Calls to action

Example Workflow: Writing a Blog Post with AI

Topic: Best Morning Routines for Productivity

1. Generate Outline (ChatGPT)
Prompt:

"Create a detailed blog post outline for the topic: 'Best Morning Routines for Productivity.' Include H2 and H3 headings."

2. Expand into Draft (ChatGPT)
Prompt:

"Write a 1,200-word blog post based on this outline. Use a friendly, conversational tone. Optimize for SEO keywords: morning routine, productivity tips, daily habits."

3. Polish & Humanize

- Edit in Grammarly/Quillbot.
- Add personal examples or stories (this makes it relatable).

4. Add Images (Canva, Unsplash, or MidJourney)
Prompt for MidJourney:

"Minimalist illustration of a person meditating at sunrise, digital art."

5. SEO Optimization (SurferSEO or NeuronWriter)

- Check keywords, readability, and structure.

AI Prompt Box – SEO Optimizer

Ask ChatGPT:

"Rewrite this blog introduction to be more engaging and SEO-friendly. Add the keyword 'morning productivity tips' naturally."

Scaling with AI

Once you know the process, you can create **5–10 blog posts per month** with AI assistance. In 6 months, you'll have 30–50 posts working for you like little "digital employees."

👉 Pro tip: Use AI to repurpose content.

- Blog → YouTube script → Instagram carousel → Email newsletter.

Real Example

Maya, a stay-at-home mom, started a blog about **healthy lunchbox recipes**. She used ChatGPT to generate recipe posts and Canva for images. After 4 months, her blog reached **15,000 monthly visitors**.

- Income: \$250 from ads + \$400 from affiliate links (lunchboxes, kitchen gadgets).
- She now has a part-time income from home.

Her secret? **Consistency + AI-powered writing.**

💡 **AI Prompt Box – 30 Blog Post Ideas**
Ask ChatGPT:

"Generate 30 blog post ideas for a new blog about \[your niche]. Make sure they are SEO-friendly and likely to get search traffic."

Chapter Summary

- Blogging is still powerful for passive income in 2025.
- Monetization comes from ads, affiliates, products, and email lists.
- AI helps with **niche research, outlines, drafts, SEO, and repurposing content.**
- Start with 5–10 posts and scale consistently.
- Combine AI efficiency with your **human touch** (stories, opinions, examples).

Chapter 6: Ebooks & Digital Products with AI

Why Digital Products Are the Ultimate Side Hustle

Imagine this: you create something **once** and it sells **forever.**

That's the magic of digital products:

- No inventory.
- No shipping costs.
- 100% profit after initial creation.

With AI, anyone can create ebooks, guides, templates, or printables — even if they've never written or designed before.

Types of Digital Products You Can Create with AI

1. Ebooks – Short guides, "how-to" manuals, or story collections.

2. Workbooks / Journals – Goal planners, fitness trackers, gratitude journals.

3. Printables – Budget trackers, meal planners, wall art (Etsy loves these).

4. Templates – Canva templates, resume designs, presentation slides.

5. Mini Courses– AI helps outline lessons, scripts, and slides.

How to Create an Ebook with AI

Let's walk through a real example.

Topic:Healthy Meal Prep for Busy Professionals

1. Brainstorm Ideas

Prompt:

"Suggest 10 ebook topics about quick and healthy meals for busy professionals. Include target audience and potential chapter titles."

2. Generate Outline

Prompt:

"Create a detailed 8-chapter outline for an ebook called 'Healthy Meal Prep for Busy Professionals.' Make it practical and beginner-friendly."

3. Write Chapters (ChatGPT)

Prompt:

"Write Chapter 1 of the ebook 'Healthy Meal Prep for Busy Professionals.' Use a friendly, motivational tone. Include examples, bullet points, and action steps."

👉 Repeat for each chapter.

4. **Polish & Add Personality**

- Add your own tips, stories, or photos.
- Use Grammarly/Quillbot for final editing.

5. Design Ebook (Canva or Atticus)

- Canva → Choose an ebook template → Insert text + images.

- Export as PDF.

💡 AI Prompt Box – Ebook Formatter

Ask ChatGPT:

"Rewrite this content in a way that fits an ebook format. Add subheadings, bullet points, and an engaging summary at the end of the chapter."

Selling Your Ebook

Platforms where you can sell:

- **Amazon Kindle Direct Publishing (KDP)** – Reach millions of readers.
- **Gumroad / Payhip** – Direct sales with instant downloads.
- **Etsy**– Great for planners, journals, and printables.
- **Your own website** – Keep 100% of the profit.

Pricing:

- Short ebooks (30–50 pages): $4.99 – $9.99
- Premium guides: $19 – $49

Digital Products (Beyond Ebooks)Other

1. Printables on Etsy

- Example: Budget planner, wedding checklist, kids' activity sheets.
- AI can design these in Canva quickly.

💡 Prompt for Canva AI:

"Create a minimalist printable budget tracker for monthly expenses."

2. Canva Templates

- Social media templates, resumes, business cards.
- Sell on Etsy, Gumroad, or Creative Market.

Prompt for ChatGPT:

"Suggest 10 profitable Canva template ideas that small business owners or content creators would buy."

3. Workbooks / Journals

- Daily gratitude journal, fitness tracker, productivity planner.
- Format in Canva, sell on KDP or Etsy.

Prompt for ChatGPT:

"Generate 30 journal prompts for a self-love workbook. Make them thoughtful and inspiring."

Real Example

Sophie, a 27-year-old graphic designer, started selling **AI-created planners on Etsy**. Using ChatGPT for copywriting + Canva for design, she built 15 products in 2 months.

Her shop now earns **$1,200/month**. Most sales are from 3 bestsellers: a productivity planner, a fitness tracker, and a wedding checklist.

Her secret? **Testing different digital products until one took off.**

Chapter Summary

- Digital products = create once, sell forever.
- Ebooks, workbooks, printables, templates, and journals are all easy to create with AI.
- Use ChatGPT for **outlines, writing, prompts, and content polish**.
- Use Canva/MidJourney for design.
- Sell on KDP, Gumroad, Etsy, or your own website.

💡 AI Prompt Box – Digital Product Brainstorm

Ask ChatGPT:

"Generate 20 digital product ideas I can sell online. Include ebooks, printables, and templates. Suggest the best platform for each (Amazon KDP, Etsy, Gumroad)."

Chapter 7: AI Tools for Small Business Support

Why Small Businesses Need AI (and You)

Think about your local café, salon, or yoga studio.
They're usually:

- Too busy running daily operations.
- Short on staff.
- Unsure how to handle social media, ads, or admin tasks.

They know they need an online presence but don't have the time or budget to hire an agency.

👉 This is where **you + AI** step in.

You can become their affordable "AI-powered assistant" and charge for services they truly need.

Services You Can Offer (Powered by AI)

1. Social Media Management

- Create posts, captions, and hashtags with ChatGPT + Canva.
- Schedule posts with Buffer/Later.

💡 Prompt:

"Create a 1-month Instagram content calendar for a local coffee shop. Include post ideas, captions, and hashtags."

2. Google My Business (GMB) Optimization

- Write engaging business descriptions.
- Respond to customer reviews (AI helps make it polite & professional).

💡 Prompt:

"Write a friendly Google business description for a yoga studio. Make it 750 characters, inviting, and keyword-rich."

3. Email Marketing

- Write newsletters, promotions, and welcome emails.

Prompt:

"Write a promotional email for a bakery offering 20% off cakes this weekend. Make it short, catchy, and add a clear call-to-action."

4. Ad Copywriting

- Facebook/Instagram ads → ChatGPT generates variations.
- Google ads → AI suggests keyword-rich headlines.

Prompt:

"Write 5 Facebook ad headlines and descriptions for a local hair salon promoting a new discount package."

5. Basic Admin Support

- Replying to FAQs (AI generates polite responses).
- Summarizing reports.
- Creating invoices/templates.

💡 Prompt:

"Draft a polite response for a customer who asked if our café offers vegan breakfast options. Keep it warm and professional."

Example: Helping a Local Business

Let's say you offer to help a **small bakery**

- **Social Media:** 12 posts/month (designed in Canva + captions from ChatGPT).
- **Email Newsletter:** 1 per week.
- **Google Reviews Replies:** Handled with AI.

You charge \$200/month for this package.

If you sign just **5 businesses**, that's **$1,000/month side income** — with AI doing most of the heavy lifting.

How to Find Clients

1. Start with your **local area**: cafés, gyms, salons, shops.

2. Offer a **free sample**: "I made 3 Instagram posts for your café — want me to handle a month of content?"

3. Pitch your services as **affordable and AI-powered**.

💡 AI Prompt Box – Pitch Email

Ask ChatGPT:

"Write a short, friendly email offering social media management services to a small local business. Keep it professional but approachable. Include a free sample offer."

Real Example

John, a college student, offered to manage the social media of a **local gym**. He used ChatGPT for captions, Canva for designs, and scheduled posts via Buffer.

- Gym owner paid him **$250/month**.
- After 3 months, he signed 4 more clients (salon, dentist, café, yoga teacher).
- Now he makes **$1,250/month** part-time.

He doesn't have marketing training — his "secret weapon" is **AI + consistency**.

Chapter Summary

- Small businesses need help but can't afford big agencies.
- You can provide **AI-powered support**: social media, Google business profiles, email, ads, and admin tasks.
- Charge per month ($200–$500 per client).
- Start with free samples → convert to paying clients.
- Just 5 clients = $1,000/month.

💡 AI Prompt Box – Service Package Builder

Ask ChatGPT:

"Create 3 AI-powered service packages I can offer small businesses. Make them beginner-friendly, affordable, and easy to deliver with tools like ChatGPT, Canva, and Buffer."

Chapter 8: AI + Trading and Investing

▲ Important Disclaimer

Trading and investing always carry **financial risks**.

- AI tools can help with research, signals, and automation — but they cannot **guarantee profits.**
- Never trade with money you cannot afford to lose.
- Always start small, treat it as learning, and consider consulting a financial advisor.

How AI is Used in Trading

AI is changing the stock market, crypto, and forex by analyzing huge amounts of data faster than humans.

Some common uses:

1. Market Sentiment Analysis – AI scans news, social media, and forums to understand public mood about a stock or crypto.

2. Price Prediction Models – AI looks at patterns to suggest possible price movements.

3. Automated Trading Bots – AI executes trades automatically based on set rules.

4. Risk Management – AI suggests stop-loss levels and portfolio balance.

Popular AI-Powered Trading Tools

TradingView + AI scripts → Visualize charts and add AI indicators.

MetaTrader Bots (MT4/MT5) → Automate forex trading strategies.

Crypto Bots (Pionex, 3Commas) → Run AI-powered strategies for crypto.

FinChat / ChatGPT Plugins → Analyze financial reports in plain English.

Example: Using AI for Stock Research

Let's say you're curious about **Tesla stock**.

💡 **AI Prompt Box – Stock Analysis**

Ask ChatGPT:

"Analyze Tesla's recent financial performance and give me a summary in plain English. Include key risks and opportunities for investors."

👉 AI gives you a **human-readable breakdown** of complex financial reports.

Example: Using AI for Trading Strategies

Instead of guessing, you can ask AI for help designing rules.

AI Prompt Box – Trading Strategy Builder

"Create a beginner-friendly trading strategy for Bitcoin using moving averages (50-day and 200-day). Include clear entry and exit rules."

AI will output a strategy you can test in **paper trading (simulated environment)** before risking real money.

Crypto Bots Example

Imagine you set up a **grid bot** on Binance or Pionex:

- Bot buys Bitcoin when the price dips below $40,000.
- Bot sells when the price goes above $42,000.

The bot runs **24/7** — no emotion, no fear, no greed.
But ▲ if the market crashes hard, bots can also lose money.

AI for Long-Term Investing

Not everyone wants to day-trade. AI also helps long-term investors:

Portfolio Analysis → AI suggests how to diversify (stocks, bonds, ETFs).

Risk Assessment → AI explains what percentage of your portfolio is at risk.

Dividend Tracking → AI reminds you of payouts.

💡 AI Prompt Box – Portfolio Checkup

"I have \$10,000 to invest. Suggest a beginner-friendly portfolio with a mix of stocks, ETFs, and bonds. Keep it low-risk and explain why."

Real Example

Arjun, a 30-year-old engineer, started using an AI crypto bot with just $200.

- In his first month, he made $15 profit.
- By the third month, he scaled to $1,000.
- Some months were up, some down, but overall he was learning **how markets work** without spending hours on charts.

His secret? **He started small and treated it as education**.

Chapter Summary

- AI makes trading and investing easier by analyzing data, automating trades, and managing risk.
- Tools include **TradingView, MetaTrader bots, Pionex, 3Commas, ChatGPT financial plugins**.
- Start with **paper trading** or small amounts.
- Always remember: **AI is a tool, not a crystal ball**.
- Treat AI trading as **high risk and experimental**.

💡 AI Prompt Box – Risk Awareness

Ask ChatGPT:

"List the 10 biggest risks of using AI-powered trading bots for beginners. Suggest how to minimize these risks."

Chapter 9: Real Stories & Case Studies

Why Stories Matter

Information tells.
Stories sell.

Up until now, you've seen strategies and prompts. But here's the truth: you don't need to be a genius, a coder, or a social media celebrity. Real people — students, parents, employees, retirees — are using AI for extra income.

Let's meet a few of them.

Case Study 1: The Student Freelancer

Name: Riya (21, India)
Background: College student in business studies.

Riya wanted to earn pocket money but didn't know where to start. She discovered Fiverr and decided to offer **blog writing with AI assistance**.

Her Process:

- She used ChatGPT to generate blog drafts.
- Added her own editing + personality.
- Delivered posts in 24 hours (faster than most freelancers).

Results:

- First order: $15 for a 1,000-word blog.

- After 2 months: averaging \$400/month.
- Her edge = "fast delivery + affordable pricing," made possible by AI.

💡 **Lesson:** AI made her competitive even as a beginner.

Case Study 2: The Stay-at-Home Mom on Etsy

Name: Sophie (27, USA)
Background: Graphic designer turned mom.

Sophie wanted a flexible income. She started selling **AI-designed planners and journals** on Etsy.

Her Process:

- ChatGPT for journal prompts.
- Canva AI for design.
- Uploaded 10 products to Etsy.

Results:

- First sale within 2 weeks: $7.
- After 3 months: ~ $1,200/month.
- Top seller = Productivity Planner & Fitness Tracker.

Lesson: Digital products = passive income. She works 2–3 hours/week now.

Case Study 3: The Motivational YouTuber

Name: David (19, UK)
Background: University student, no video editing skills.

David wanted to try YouTube Shorts but had no idea how to make videos. He used AI to create **motivational content**.

His Process:

- ChatGPT → 30-second motivational scripts.
- Pexels (free stock video) + CapCut captions.
- AI voiceover with ElevenLabs.

Results:

- First month: 50 subscribers.
- After 3 months: 10,000+ subscribers.
- Income: \~\$400/month from ads + affiliate links.

💡 **Lesson:** Consistency + AI shortcuts can grow an audience fast.

Case Study 4: The Local Business Helper

Name: John (23, Canada)
Background: Part-time student, loves tech.

John noticed his local gym's Instagram looked dead. He offered to help for $250/month.

His Process:

- ChatGPT → captions & ad copy.
- Canva → posts & stories.
- Buffer → scheduling.

Results:

- Gym signed him.
- Then he signed 4 more businesses (dentist, café, salon, yoga teacher).
- Income: ~ $1,250/month part-time.

💡 **Lesson:** Small businesses are eager for affordable AI-powered support.

Case Study 5: The Curious Crypto Trader

Name: Arjun (30, India)
Background: IT engineer, curious about crypto.

Arjun wanted to test AI trading bots.

His Process:

- Started with $200 on a crypto bot (Pionex).
- AI bot ran grid trades 24/7.
- Used ChatGPT to learn trading strategies.

Results:

- Made $15 profit first month.
- Gradually scaled to $1,000 capital.
- Some months profitable, some not.
- He treats it as a **learning tool**, not guaranteed income.

💡 **Lesson:** AI trading is experimental. Start small, learn, and never risk what you can't afford.

What These Stories Prove

You don't need to be an expert.

You don't need huge capital.

AI gives **ordinary people superpowers** to create income streams.

The common factor? **Action + Consistency**.

AI Prompt Box – Case Study Explorer

Ask ChatGPT:

"Give me 5 success stories of people making side income with AI in 2024–2025. Summarize how they did it and what tools they used."

This way, you can keep yourself motivated with real-world inspiration.

Chapter Summary

- Real people (students, moms, employees, entrepreneurs) are making extra income with AI.
- Their methods range from freelancing → Etsy → YouTube → business services → trading.
- The secret isn't talent or money — it's **starting small, using AI as leverage, and staying consistent.**

Appendix: Your Quick AI Toolkit

Here's a curated list of AI tools, platforms, and resources mentioned throughout this book. Think of it as your **side income starter pack**.

✍ Content Writing & Blogging ✍

ChatGPT / Claude → Draft blog posts, social media content, SEO articles.

Jasper AI → Professional AI writer with templates.

Copy.ai → Marketing-focused AI content generator.

Grammarly → Proofreading & editing assistant.

💡 Prompt Example:

"Write a 1,000-word blog post on '5 Tips for Healthy Remote Work Habits.' Make it conversational, SEO-friendly, and include a catchy intro + conclusion."

🎨 Graphic Design & Digital Products

Canva (with AI features) → Templates, social media posts, ebooks.

Kittl → Advanced AI design tool for print-on-demand.

MidJourney / DALL·E → Create stunning AI art and product visuals.

Creative Fabrica Spark → AI-generated fonts, graphics, and designs.

Prompt Example (MidJourney):

“A cozy minimalist watercolor illustration of a coffee cup with books on a wooden table, warm pastel colors, suitable for a journal cover.”

🎥 Video Creation & Voiceovers

Pictory AI → Turn text into videos automatically.

Runway AI → Video editing + AI special effects.

CapCut / VEED.io → Quick editing with captions and effects.

ElevenLabs / Murf AI → Human-like AI voiceovers.

💡 Prompt Example (ChatGPT for video script):

“Write a 30-second motivational video script for YouTube Shorts. The theme: never give up, use strong emotional words, and end with a call to action.”

E-Commerce & Print-on-Demand

Etsy → Sell digital products (planners, journals, templates).

Redbubble / Teespring → Sell AI-designed merch.

Printify / Printful → Print-on-demand services connected to Shopify.

KDP (Amazon Kindle Publishing) → Sell ebooks created with AI help.

Prompt Example (ChatGPT for Etsy):

“Generate 20 unique gratitude journal prompts for women, short and uplifting, to include in a printable journal for Etsy.”

💼 Freelancing & Online Gigs

Fiverr / Upwork / Freelancer → Offer services like writing, social media, design.

PeoplePerHour → UK-based freelancing marketplace.

Contra → Freelance platform with 0% commission.

💡 Prompt Example (Gig Description):

Write a Fiverr gig description for a service: I create SEO-friendly blog posts using AI tools and human editing. Highlight fast delivery, affordability, and originality.”

■ Trading & Finance Tools

TradingView → AI-powered indicators and stock/crypto charts.

Pionex / 3Commas → AI-driven crypto trading bots.

MetaTrader (MT4/MT5) → Forex trading automation.

FinChat / ChatGPT Plugins → Summarize financial reports.

Prompt Example:

“Explain Tesla’s last quarterly report in plain English. Highlight revenue growth, risks, and future opportunities.”

Automation & Productivity

Zapier → Connect apps and automate workflows.

Notion AI → Organize tasks, notes, and AI summaries.

Otter.ai → AI meeting transcriptions.

ChatGPT Plugins / Extensions → Supercharge your workflow (e.g., SEO plugin, research plugin).

💡 Prompt Example (Notion AI):

"Summarize my weekly to-do list into a 3-day action plan with priority tasks."

🌐 Learning & Growth Resources

YouTube Channels: Ali Abdaal, Matt Wolfe (AI tools & side hustle guides).

Communities: Reddit r/sidehustle, Indie Hackers, ProductHunt.

Skill Platforms: Coursera, Udemy (AI + business skills).

■ Appendix Summary

This toolkit isn't about using every tool at once.

- **Pick 1–2 tools per side hustle idea.**
- **Experiment.**
- **Stay consistent.**

Over time, you'll naturally expand your toolkit — just like a carpenter adds new tools only when needed.

Chapter 10: Conclusion – Your AI Income Action Plan (60-Day Roadmap)

Why a 60-Day Plan?

Most people get stuck after learning. They feel excited but don't take consistent action. This plan is designed to:

■ Keep you moving.

Give you small wins quickly.

Build a solid foundation for long-term side income.

Phase 1: Discover & Prepare (Days 1–14)

● Goal: Explore AI tools, pick your income path, and set up basics.

Checklist:

👉 Choose 1 side hustle idea (freelancing, Etsy, YouTube, trading, etc.).

Set up required accounts (Fiverr, Etsy, YouTube, etc.).

Explore **ChatGPT + Canva** (core tools for most ideas).

Collect at least 10 example prompts you'll use often.

Create your "AI Side Income Journal" (Notion/Google Docs) to track progress.

Tip: Don't overthink. Just pick one path you feel excited about.

Phase 2: Create & Launch (Days 15–30)

● Goal: Build your first real product/service and go live.

Checklist:

👉Write your first gig description (if freelancing).

Create 1 digital product (if Etsy or KDP).

Make 3 sample posts/videos (if YouTube/social media).

Run at least 1 AI-powered experiment (blog, video, design).

Publish your first offer online.

Tip: Don't wait for perfection. Your first product/service is your practice ground.

Phase 3: Promote & Get First Wins (Days 31–45)

Goal: Get visibility, land your first sale/client/viewers.

Checklist:

Share your service/product on 3 platforms (social media, forums, groups).

Use AI to write outreach messages for potential clients.

Create a simple marketing plan (2 posts per week).

👉Offer a "beta discount" or free sample to get reviews/testimonials.

Track what works (did you get clicks, views, messages?).

Tip: Focus on momentum, not money. First $1 = proof it works.

Phase 4: Scale & Optimize (Days 46–60)

🎯 Goal: Grow from small wins into a repeatable system.

Checklist:

Analyze your results (which product/gig/post worked best?).

Double down on what's working — drop what isn't.

Use AI for automation (schedule posts, batch content, repurpose).

Create at least 3 more offers or products.

Plan your **next 90 days** with improved strategy.

Tip: Success is about iteration. Use AI to multiply your efforts, not to shortcut consistency.

🚀 Final Words

By following this roadmap, in just 60 days you will:

- Have chosen a side hustle path.
- Published your first AI-powered product/service.
- Earned your **first side income win**.
- Built a foundation to scale further.

Remember: AI is your **assistant**, not your replacement.

It gives you **speed, creativity, and leverage** — but it's your consistency and vision that turn it into income.

The question isn't **"Can AI help me make side income?"**

The real question is: **"Will I take the first step and keep going?"**

www.ingramcontent.com/pod-product-compliance
Lightning Source LLC
LaVergne TN
LVHW082359200926
848481LV00012B/3626
* 9 7 9 8 2 3 2 2 4 1 7 7 3 *